I LIKE BIG BOOKS AND I CANNOT LIE

OLD-SCHOOL ROCK-AND-ROLL LIKE YOU'VE NEVER READ BEFORE!

written by
Tamara Dever

PUZZLES, GAMES, TRIVIA, AND LYRICAL FUN LINKING LITERARY CLASSICS
WITH '70S AND '80S POP AND ROCK CLASSICS

NARROW GATE
BOOKS
Austin, Texas

CRAZY FOR YOU

For all of my fellow self-proclaimed book and music geeks.
*Be **Overjoyed** because it's still **Hip to be Square**.*

Narrow Gate Books
NarrowGateBooks.com, Austin, Texas

Book cover and interior design © TLC Book Design, *TLCBookDesign.com*

ISBN: 978-0-9987023-2-2

Where Do We Go FROM HERE?

WE'RE IN THIS LOVE *Together*

Do you stand in line like a **Fool in the Rain** to buy the latest bestseller? Are you **Walking on Sunshine** when you finally buy it?

Authors, are you **Too Shy** to market your book or are you waiting for the day when **Everybody Wants You** to talk about your book on their show?

If your favorite pastimes include reading and listening to '70s and '80s music, you're going to have a blast with this book. (If not, **Run, Runaway**.) It will make you laugh, smile, and maybe even roll your eyes while doing so. It will test your knowledge of books, their authors, and classic rock and pop songs and their artists.

On the pages within, you'll find trivia, brainteasers, quizzes, crossword puzzles, and many songs you'll recognize—sort of. You see, the tunes haven't changed, but the words have! Each remastered song now has a book-related theme and you'll never hear it **Just the Same Way** again. If you can't quite remember how a melody goes, visit ILikeBigBooks.com for a link to our YouTube channel featuring a playlist with the songs in the order they appear in this book. The songs

in this book are presented in themed groups that begin with a simple love of reading and proceed to follow the process of publishing a book. If you're a reader, but not in the publishing industry, you may learn a little about the journey books take to get into your hands.

Within the games, you'll find book titles in *italics* to help differentiate from the song titles. The songs and artists are predominantly from the '80s with a sprinkling of some from the '70s. Books and authors span many decades, but are either classics or have been on a bestseller list at some point. If you get stuck, **Don't Worry, Be Happy**. There's an answer key in the back!

In the end, my **Desire** is that this book will entertain you. May it bring you laughter, inspire you to share something funny with a friend, and perhaps even inspire you to write your own music or book.

Thank you for geeking out with me over a shared love of words and music. **After All**, **We're In This Love Together**! And **Don't Stop 'Til You Get Enough.**

Let the Music Play,

Jami

Tamara Dever, CEO of TLC Book Design and lifelong music lover

READY OR NOT

(Are you ready?)

LET'S GO

I mean it—

COME ON, LET'S GO

because

**NOTHING'S GOING
TO STOP US NOW**

DOES YOUR

Mother Know?

SONGS THAT MENTION
OR REFERENCE BOOKS

*Bet you didn't realize rock and pop musicians
could be so well-read!*

SONGS WITH TITLES THAT MENTION BOOK TITLES

BOOK: *1984* **by George Orwell**

SONGS: 1984 and Big Brother, David Bowie

Bowie wrote many songs inspired by this classic novel.

BOOK: *Atrocity Exhibition* **by JG Ballard**

SONG: Atrocity Exhibition, Joy Division

BOOK: *Beyond the Wall of Sleep* **(short story) by H. P. Lovecraft**

SONG: Behind the Wall of Sleep, Black Sabbath

BOOK: *For Whom The Bell Tolls* **by Ernest Hemingway**

SONG: For Whom The Bell Tolls, Metallica

BOOK: *Frankenstein* **by Mary Shelley**

SONG: Feed My Frankenstein, Alice Cooper

BOOK: *The House at Pooh Corner* **by A. A. Milne**

SONGS: House at Pooh Corner and Return to Pooh Corner, Kenny Loggins

---

BOOK: *Lord of the Flies* **by William Golding**

SONG: Lord of the Flies, Iron Maiden

BOOK: *Pet Sematary* **by Stephen King**

SONG: Pet Sematary, Ramones

BOOK: *The Rocket Man*, **a short story in the book** *The Illustrated Man* **by Ray Bradbury**

SONGS: Rocket Man, Elton John and Rocket Man, Pearls Before Swine

---

BOOK: *The Sheltering Sky* **by Paul Bowles**

SONG: The Sheltering Sky, King Crimson

BOOK: *Tarzan of the Apes* **by Edgar Rice Burroughs**

SONG: Tarzan Boy, Baltimora

BOOK: *Uncle Tom's Cabin* **by Harriet Beecher Stowe**

SONG: Uncle Tom's Cabin, Warrant

BOOK: *Yertle The Turtle* **by Dr. Seuss**

SONG: Yertle The Turtle, Red Hot Chili Peppers

This may be the funkiest version of a Dr. Seuss story ever!

SONGS INSPIRED BY SPECIFIC BOOKS

BOOK: *Alice's Adventures in Wonderland* **by Lewis Caroll**

SONGS: I am the Walrus, The Beatles and The Wanderer, Donna Summer

---

BOOK: *The Bourne Identity* **by Robert Ludlum**

SONG: Twilight Zone, Golden Earring

Surprisingly, the song was inspired by this book, not the TV show.*

BOOK: *Dune* **by Frank Herbert**

SONG: To Tame a Land, Iron Maiden

Herbert hated rock bands and would not allow the band to title this song after his novel.*

BOOK: *The Iliad* **by Homer**

SONG: Cassandra, ABBA

This song is about its title character from Homer's book.

BOOK: *The Inheritors* **by William Golding**

SONG: A Trick of the Tail, Genesis

BOOK: *Interview with the Vampire* **by Anne Rice**

SONG: Moon over Bourbon Street, Sting

About a character in Rice's book.

BOOK: *Johnny Got His Gun* **by Dalton Trumbo**

SONG: One, Metallica

BOOK: *Lolita*
by Vladimir Nabokov
SONG: Don't Stand So
Close to Me, The Police
The song refers to "that book by Nabokov."

BOOK: *Lord of the Flies*
by William Golding
SONG: Shadows and
Tall Trees, U2
The song shares a title with a chapter of the book.

BOOK: *On the Beach*
by Nevil Shute
SONG: Everyday Is Like Sunday,
Morrissey
Morrissey was lyrically inspired by this novel while writing the song.*

BOOK: *One Flew Over the
Cuckoo's Nest* **by Ken Kesey**
SONG: Take Me Home,
Phil Collins
This song is about a man in a mental institution, not about someone returning home.*

BOOK: *The Sheltering Sky*
by Paul Bowles
SONG: Tea in the Sahara,
The Police
The song is named for just a single chapter of this novel.*

BOOK: *The Stand*
by Stephen King
SONG: Among the Living,
Anthrax

BOOK: *Still Life With
Woodpecker*
by Tom Robbins
SONG: Make Love Stay,
Dan Fogelberg

BOOK: *Through the
Looking-Glass*
by Lewis Carroll
SONG: Lucy in the Sky with
Diamonds, The Beatles

BOOK: *Triad* **by Mary Leader**
SONG: Rhiannon, Fleetwood Mac
Titled and written about a female character in the book.*

Finally…

WE DIDN'T START THE FIRE

This hit from Billy Joel mentions a combination of ten book titles and author names! In order, they are:

The Catcher in the Rye (by J. D. Salinger)

Peter Pan (by J. M. Barrie)
> *Though the song likely refers to the*
> *Broadway play, it was also a book.*

Peyton Place (by Grace Metalious)

(Boris) Pasternak

(Jack) Kerouac

Bridge on the River Kwai (by Pierre Boulle)
> *The movie was based on the book.*

Ben-Hur (by Lew Wallace)
> *Again, the movie was based on the book.*

Psycho (by Robert Bloch)
> *Yup, the movie was based on the book.*

(Ernest) Hemingway

Stranger In A Strange Land
    (by Robert A. Heinlein)

From www.songfacts.com | Other resources: https://bookriot.com/2016/07/26/29-popular-songs-reference-classic-books/ and www.shortlist.com/entertainment/music/25-songs-that-reference-books/78348

WORD *Up*

SONGS WHOSE TITLES REPRESENT GENRES OF FICTION

New **Romance** (It's a **Mystery**) by Spider

A Little **Romance** by The Boys

History Never Repeats by Split Enz

Thriller by Michael Jackson

It's No **Crime** by Babyface

Different Story (World Of Lust And **Crime**) by Peter Schilling

I Want **Action** by Poison

Words Into **Action** by Jermaine Jackson

Fantasy by Aldo Nova

My **Fantasy** by Teddy Riley

This One's For The **Children** by New Kids On The Block

FOR THOSE WHO SIMPLY

LOVE BOOKS

*SONGS ABOUT READING, OWNING
AND BEING OBSESSED WITH
LITERARY WORKS*

You believe the longer the book, the better the story.
Les Miserables and *Harry Potter* don't scare you!
This song will resonate with your soul.

TO THE TUNE OF

BABY GOT BACK
SIR MIX-A-LOT

I like big books and I cannot lie
You other authors can't deny
When a geek walks in with a giant tome
Or a textbook in your face
Then your tongue, gets tied in knots
And you know that text is hot

Deep in the book I'm pleading
I'm hooked and I can't stop reading
Oh baby, throughout the ages
I've come to love your pages

Librarians tried to warn me
But that big book informs me
From Rumpelstiltskin
To the length of War and Peace

I like 'em heavy, I like 'em hot
I like 'em with a really good plot
I love Lewis Carroll;
When I carry it in a wheelbarrow

You know what I'm talkin' about
Big books are back! Big books are back!

This rewrite is a tribute to those of you who value reading books above pretty much anything else.

TO THE TUNE OF

TIME AFTER TIME
CYNDI LAUPER

Lying in our bed, I hear the clock, don't think of you
Caught up, book's not dull
Conclusion is something new
Flashback, long nights, you were left behind
Bookcase of treasuries, tome after—
Sometimes you reach for me
I'm reading too far ahead
You're calling to me
I don't care what you've said
Then you say, "I'll go.
You're so unkind.
Books have you so entwined."

If I'm gone you can look—
and you'll find me in
tome after tome
If you call I won't answer—
I'll be reading
tome after tome

An ode to people like me who remember beloved books of your youth and never let go, maybe even gaining a career in publishing.

TO THE TUNE OF

SUMMER OF '69
BRYAN ADAMS

I got my first real mystery
Bought it at the five and dime
Read it till my eyes were red
Was the summer of '89.

Read Hardy Boys in school
During band, even while in art
Nearly quit from being harried
Friends just moan, saying "You're bizarre."
But when I look back now
Those stories seemed to last forever
And in my own voice
Yeah, I became a writer
Those were the best days of my life.

If you're bookish to the nth degree,
be yourself and let your geek flag fly!

SUPERFREAK
RICK JAMES

She's a very bookish girl,
She loves the ISBN numbers;
She will never put her fiction down,
Once she buys it, that's so sweet!

She likes Tolstoy and Ayn Rand,
She says that I'm her all-time favorite;
When she takes my novel to her room, it's the night time;
she says it's the bee's knees.

That girl is pretty mild now;
The girl's a super geek;
The kind of girl you read about
in *Library Magazine*.
That girl is pretty inky;
The girl's a super geek;
I really write to please her
She tells me that I'm neat.

She's all right; she's all right / That girl's all right with me yeah.
She's a super geek, super geek
She's super geeky; Yow / Super geek, super geek.
She's super geeky; Yow

WE GO TOGETHER

In this game, you'll find a book title (in italics) and a song title, both missing a word they have in common. Fill in the blank and, if you're feeling extra smart, list the book's author and song's performer for extra credit.

HINT: Books are bestsellers from various decades. Songs are from the '70s and '80s.

FOR EXAMPLE: *The Shining* and "Shining Star"

The ____ Shining ____ Star

Book's author ____ Stephen King ____

Song performed by ____ Earth, Wind, and Fire ____

1) She's a _____ *and the Beast*

   Book's author _____

   Song performed by _____

2) *All Creatures Great and* _____ Town

   Book's author _____

   Song performed by _____

3) Welcome to the _____*Book*

   Book's author _____

   Song performed by _____

4) *Think and Grow* _____Girl

   Book's author _____

   Song performed by _____

5) You Don't Bring Me _____*in the Attic*

   Book's author _____

   Song performed by _____

6) *Watership* _____Under

   Book's author _____

   Song performed by _____

A Little Bit More…

7) Already _____ *With the Wind*

   Book's author _____

   Song performed by _____

8) *The Hunger* _____ People Play

   Book's author _____

   Song performed by _____

9) *The Fault in Our* _____ On 45 Medley

   Book's author _____

   Song performed by _____

10) *The Girl on the* _____ in Vain

    Book's author _____

    Song performed by _____

11) Party _____ *Farm*

Book's author _____

Song performed by _____

12) Foolish _____ *and Prejudice*

Book's author _____

Song performed by _____

13) *The* _____ of My Success

Book's author _____

Song performed by _____

14) You Light Up My _____ *of Pi*

Book's author _____

Song performed by _____

Answers on page 95.

THE LOGICAL SONG

Let's assume for a few minutes that each of these musical artists
is an author. Now let's get into their heads and determine
how they might fill in these blanks.

HINT: All answers are song titles.

1) What the Eurythmics are thinking when they win their first award:

_____ _____ (_____ _____

_____ _____).

2) When Gino Vannelli fails to write a bestseller after five tries, he declares:

"____ _____ _____ _____."

3) What Sheena Easton says when asked how she likes the book she's reading:

"_____ _____ _____ _____."

4) What Simple Minds says when their novel falls off of the bestseller list:

"_____ _____ _____ _____ _____."

5) How the Cars get to their book signings: They _____.

6) Disappointed, Genesis gets this after sending their manuscript to multiple agents for consideration: "_____ _____ _____ _____."

7) What an emotional Stevie Wonder says to his adored publisher:

"____ _____ _____ _____ _____ ____

_____ _____."

8) What Styx says when they have a streak of bestselling books:

"_____ _____ _____ _____."

9) What Richard Marx said to himself after releasing his book without hiring a professional editor first: "_____ _____ _____."

10) What Rick Astley says when asking for book reviews:

"_____ _____ _____ _____ _____."

Answers on page 95.

Dr. Feelgood

*If rock/pop stars wrote health and medical books,
what would they be titled?*

AILMENTS

EXAMPLES: Blind Vision: Blancmange | **Broken**: Tears For Fears

Now it's your turn!

SONG	ARTIST

A Little Bit More…

HOW I'M FEELING

EXAMPLES: I Can Survive: Triumph | **King of Pain:** The Police

Now it's your turn!

SONG   ARTIST

_____   _____

_____   _____

_____   _____

_____   _____

_____   _____

_____   _____

_____   _____

_____   _____

_____   _____

_____   _____

_____   _____

_____   _____

CRIES FOR HELP

EXAMPLES: Emergency: Kool & The Gang | **Rescue Me:** Al B. Sure!

Now it's your turn!

SONG   ARTIST

_____   _____

_____   _____

_____   _____

_____   _____

_____   _____

_____   _____

_____   _____

_____   _____

_____   _____

_____   _____

A Little Bit More…

TREATMENTS

EXAMPLES: Lifeline: Spandau Ballet | **Sexual Healing:** Marvin Gaye

Now it's your turn!

SONG   ARTIST

_____   _____

_____   _____

_____   _____

_____   _____

_____   _____

_____   _____

GENERAL MEDICAL TERMS

EXAMPLES: Alive And Kicking: Simple Minds | **Heartbeat City:** The Cars

Now it's your turn!

SONG   ARTIST

_____   _____

_____   _____

_____   _____

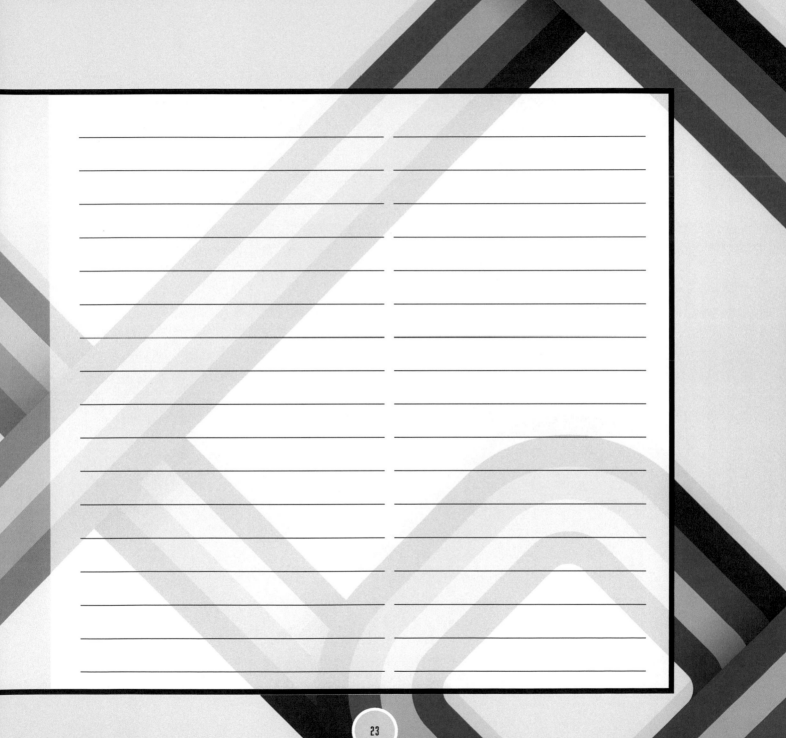

Crossroads

ACROSS

1) The librarian in the hometown of 'Til Tuesday hushes them because Voices _____.

2) Bruce Hornsby & The Range's book about the weather is about Mandolin _____.

4) Talking Heads proclaimed that meeting their favorite author was a _____ in a Lifetime experience.

6) Simply Red can't print five thousand copies of their book because Money's Too _____ to Mention

7) No publisher will sign Joan Jett because she has a Bad _____.

9) Rebbie Jackson's children's book about a bug who wears many shoes is called _____.

10) The Steve Miller Band gets to their book signings on a _____ Airliner.

11) U2's song, "40," was inspired by a verse in this book of the Bible.

DOWN

1) The B-52's are writing a sci-fi novel about an alien from Planet _____.

3) How long Kenny Loggins said it seemed to take to write his novel.

5) The Commodores' most productive time to write is during the _____.

8) Excitedly, INXS announced that their recently released bestselling thriller is a _____ Sensation.

9) Kool and the Gang hopes you will always _____ your copy of their classic book.

Answers on pages 95–96.

25

Sign YOUR NAME

The Black Crowes were originally called
Mr. Crowe's Garden, after a loved children's book.
At the suggestion of a producer in 1989,
they renamed the group.

MYSTERY

https://en.wikipedia.org/wiki/List_of_band_name_etymologies

THRILLS AND WOES

OF WRITING

SONGS ABOUT THE SOMETIMES REWARDING,
SOMETIMES MADDENING PROCESS
OF WRITING A BOOK.

Writing books calls for often untimely inspiration, determination, and a little caffeine.

PIANO MAN
BILLY JOEL

It's nine o'clock on a Saturday.
The foreword and intro are in.
There's my wife lying next to me
Beggin' me to quit and turn in.

I say, "Girl, this sure feels like treachery.
I'm not sure how to write this prose.
It's sad and it's sweet,
But it's so incomplete
I just need a few more espressos."

La de dah ditty dah. When will this darn thing be done?

I write so long; I'm a verbose man.
I'll be at it long into the night.
Though I'm not one who excels in brevity,
my editor makes it alright.

La de dah ditty dah. When will this darn thing be done?

Many books are cowritten by two or more authors.
This one's being updated for a new-and-improved edition.

TO THE TUNE OF

ICE, ICE, BABY
VANILLA ICE

Yo, VIP, let's kick it!
Write, write, Baby; write, write, Baby
All right stop, collaborate on fiction
We are back with a brand-new edition.

Nothing grabs ahold of me tritely
Write with each other daily and nightly
Will it ever stop? Yo, I don't know.

Working all night, yeah, we do so
We're reprinting; sure don't want to panhandle
Fill up a page and tell the chump
not to ramble.

The poor writer in this song has lost his way and is feeling pretty down. Many authors go through this from time to time. Hope this guy snaps out of it soon!

BOHEMIAN RHAPSODY
QUEEN

TO THE TUNE OF

Is this a romance?
Is this just fantasy?
Writing a novel,
to escape from reality.
Look at my eyes, so tired I can barely see.
I'm just an author, I need some sympathy.
The words are easy come, easy go,
he says "yes," she says "no."
Any way this plot blows, it's all really
chatter to me, whoopee.

Mama, just killed a man.
With my pencil full of lead, wrote some words and now he's dead.
Mama, the story'd just begun
But now I've gone and blown it all away.
Mama, ooh, this whole scene will make you cry,
I had a knack but now it brings such sorrow.
Writing's done, my talent's gone. I guess nothing really matters.
Nothing really matters to me.

Any way this plot blows.

Sign YOUR NAME

A line in the Anthony Burgess novel
A Clockwork Orange inspired the
name of the band Heaven 17.
In it, a character mentions
a fictional band called
The Heaven Seventeen
during a conversation in a record store.

https://en.wikipedia.org/wiki/List_of_band_name_etymologies

Here's a little pep talk for a budding author.

DON'T STOP BELIEVIN'
JOURNEY

TO THE TUNE OF

Don't have a meltdown, girl
Writin' is a lonely world
Though you're no Mark Twain
You deserve fanfare
You are more like Tolstoy
With words you are adroit
Your book is not in vain
You'll be a millionaire!

Don't stop believin'
See it to completion
Sweet plight, gleeful
Ah, ah, ahhh

This author has created a pen name, Rachel, and is quite proud of her accomplishments. ;)

TO THE TUNE OF

CENTERFOLD
J. GEILS BAND

Come on

Does she mock writer's block?
Does she mock defeat?
My nom de plume, Rachel
With perfection is replete

She's so pure, no mistakes
As no one could ever feign.
The exemplary tome by Rachel
Could never cause me pain

Fears go by, I'm feelin' new, a real writing queen.
And it's my nom de plume Rachel earning wages I've foreseen.

Lo and behold,
My new story has just been sold.
My pages have just turned to gold.
(Pages have just turned to gold.)

THE LOGICAL SONG

Let's assume for a few minutes that each of these musical artists is an author. Now let's get into their heads and determine how they might fill in these blanks.

Hint: All answers are song titles.

1) What the Thompson Twins' book would say if it were lying on the nightstand waiting to be read: "_____ _____ _____."

2) What John Lennon would say while getting ready to work on his second draft: "It's (_____ _____) _____ _____."

3) What Ray Parker Jr. says to his editor when he disagrees with his suggestion: "_____ _____ _____ _____!"

4) Who New Kids On The Block hires to design the outside of their book: A _____ _____.

5) What Queen says when they receive yet another publisher's rejection letter:

"_____ _____ _____ _____ _____."

6) What David Coverdale of Whitesnake says when he's ready to publish his second book: "_____ ____ _____ _____."

7) What Willie Nelson says when he's about to embark on another book tour: "I guess I'll be _____ _____ _____ _____."

8) How the Little River Band responds when their designer shows them a redesigned book cover. "That's a _____ _____!"

9) What an unpublished book by Wilson Philips would say:

"Please _____ _____."

10) What a library book by Eddie Money is thinking as it nears closing time:

_____ _____ _____ _____.

Answers on page 96.

WHAT A

Wonderful

WORLD

If rock/pop stars wrote nature books, what would they be titled?

ANIMALS

EXAMPLES: Batdance: Prince | **Eye of the Tiger:** Survivor | **Songbird:** Kenny G

Now it's your turn!

SONG   ARTIST

_____   _____

_____   _____

_____   _____

_____   _____

_____   _____

_____
_____
_____
_____
_____
_____
_____
_____
_____
_____
_____
_____
_____
_____

A Little Bit More…

PLANTS

EXAMPLES: A Forest: The Cure | **Touch A Four Leaf Clover:** Atlantic Starr

Now it's your turn!

SONG   ARTIST

_____   _____

_____   _____

_____   _____

_____   _____

_____   _____

_____   _____

_____   _____

_____   _____

_____   _____

_____   _____

_____   _____

_____   _____

NATURAL WONDERS

EXAMPLES: **Fire Lake:** Bob Seger | **Seven Seas of Rhye:** Queen

Now it's your turn!

SONG   ARTIST

_____   _____

_____   _____

_____   _____

_____   _____

_____   _____

_____   _____

_____   _____

_____   _____

_____   _____

_____   _____

_____   _____

Crossroads

ACROSS

1) Elton John says this seems to be the hardest word.

2) The main character in Lionel Richie's book would likely begin a conversation with this.

4) Jimmy _____, guitarist and founder of Led Zeppelin.

5) Oingo Boingo writes weird books on this topic.

8) This George would give someone just one more try at becoming a successful writer.

9) Limahl wants the story to be never-_____.

10) When Glass Tiger says they'll release their next book.

12) Starship's favorite novel might be written by this Eyre.

DOWN

1) The heroine Karyn White would write a graphic novel about.

3) How Stevie Wonder feels about getting a five-star review for his biography.

6) Squeeze needs this black drink in bed while writing.

7) REM's favorite comic book.

11) We couldn't write a thing without Prince's street of this name.

Answers on page 96.

Somebody's WATCHING ME

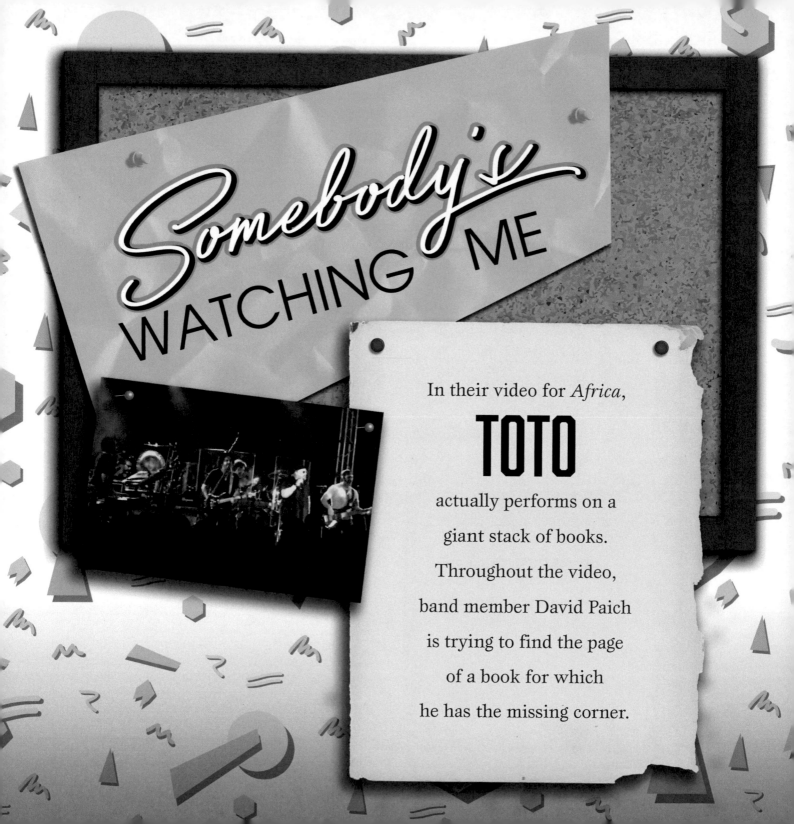

In their video for *Africa*,

TOTO

actually performs on a
giant stack of books.
Throughout the video,
band member David Paich
is trying to find the page
of a book for which
he has the missing corner.

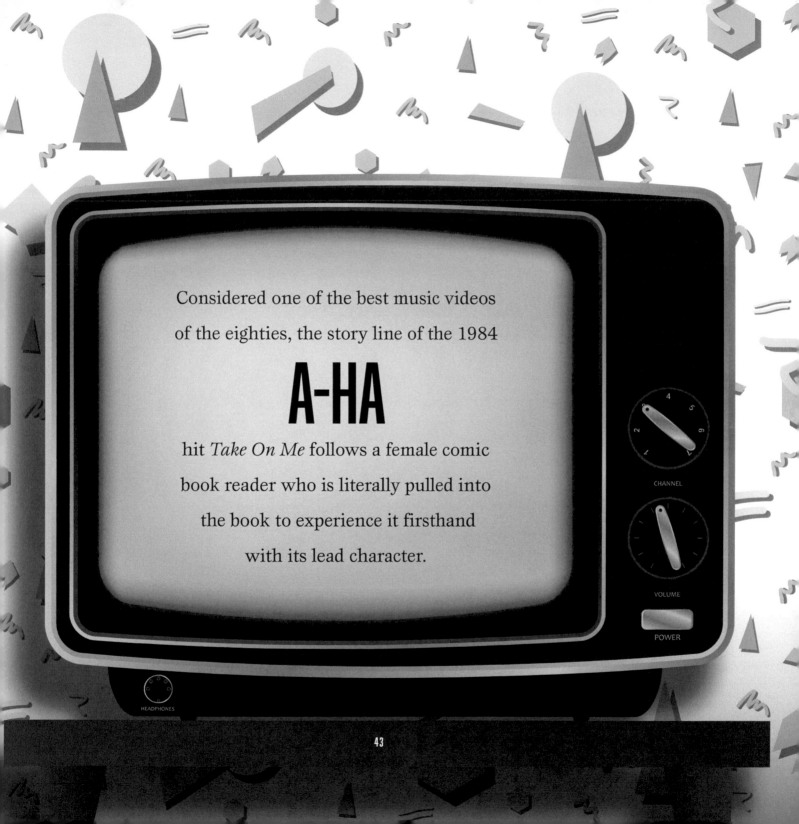

Considered one of the best music videos of the eighties, the story line of the 1984

A-HA

hit *Take On Me* follows a female comic book reader who is literally pulled into the book to experience it firsthand with its lead character.

CHANNEL

VOLUME

POWER

HEADPHONES

WORD *Up*

SONGS WITH PUBLISHING-RELATED TITLES

Between the Sheets by The Isley Brothers
We're talking about sheets of paper, people.

Paper and Fire by John Mellencamp

Press by Paul McCartney

Read 'em and Weep by Barry Manilow

Signed in Your Book of Love by Company B

Sign Your Name by Terence Trent D'Arby

Has Anyone Ever Written Anything For You by Stevie Nicks

Sequel by Harry Chapin

THE PROCESS OF

PUBLISHING

IT TAKES DESIGN, EDITING, PROOFREADING, AND PRINTING TO TURN A MANUSCRIPT INTO A BOOK.

The dream of many authors, of course, is to have a bestseller.
In the midst of his writing struggle, this writer stops
to daydream. Perhaps it will refuel him to
finish what he started.

JESSIE'S GIRL
RICK SPRINGFIELD

My brain is so spent.
Yeah, this book's takin' way too much time.
Now the ending has changed
And I drank too much wine.
The first draft is now done, but I missed the deadline.

Now I'm thinking about those highs
That I'll reach on Amazon, I just know it.
Now I'm dreaming about those charms
late, late at night.

You know I wish I had a bestseller.
I wish I had a bestseller.
Where can I find fame and fortune like that?

With a bestseller.
With retail space at a bookseller.
Where can I find fame and fortune like that?
Where can I find fame and fortune like that?

A poorly designed book cover can hinder sales and a good cover will attract readers. This song is an advertisement for a book cover designer who knows the ramifications of their work.

TO THE TUNE OF

EASY LOVER
PHIL COLLINS AND PHILIP BAILEY

Cheesy cover
It won't get sold for you, believe it.
Like no other.
Before you know it you'll be calling us, please.
We make dreamy covers.
We'll steal your heart when we reveal it.
It's like no other.
And defying heartache, you'll see.

An author's ode to their much-loved book designer, apparently found after having first dabbled with a crowd-sourcing design site.

EYE OF THE TIGER
SURVIVOR

TO THE TUNE OF

Designed it up, cover's so neat.
Took her time, she freelances.
Through persistence, front and back are complete.
It's all due to her talent and drive.

So many times it happens too fast.
You paid your cash, a sob story.
Your authorship and your dreams will not last
With design that's too cheap to survive.

It's our favorite designer;
It's the thrill of first sight.
The new cover she gave us is an eyeful.
We didn't hire her from Fiverr.
This time we did it right.
Now our cover's so great 'cause of our...our designer!

Sign YOUR NAME

A line in Arthur Janov's book

Prisoners of Pain

gave Tears for Fears their name.

P.O.D. stands for print on demand and is a simple, inexpensive way for authors to print books one at a time and as they're ordered. This means no large quantities of books to store in the basement or pay for up front.

MONEY FOR NOTHIN'
DIRE STRAITS

TO THE TUNE OF

I want my, I want my P.O.D. (4X)

Now look at them book pros, that's the way you do it
You print your book via P.O.D.
That ain't workin' that's the way you do it;
Money for nothin' and the upload's free.
Money for nothin' and the upload's free.

Now that ain't workin', that's the way you do it.
Lemme tell ya, print wise, my son.
I tell ya it's the mister at your online printer.
Yeah, he gets your editions all done.

He got a phone call, pushin' the buttons
Custom fiction or mysteries.
We got to use these print operators.
We got to use these VIPs.

This guy may need to find a new career.
Or a new editor.

DOWN UNDER
MEN AT WORK

TO THE TUNE OF

Writing started as a hobby.
I'm not quippy; I am kinda sloppy.
Editor maybe, yeah, she did me a service.
She used her pen and did an edit.
And she said:

You've succumbed to a bland noun blunder.
Where written woe transcend wonder.
Can't endear to Shakespeare, you're asunder.

Trying hard to understand her puzzles,
I pause. This is a chore and full of struggles.
I said, "It's so bleak, my language!"
She just smiled and said to rewrite or vanish.
And she said:

I'm numb from your bland noun blunder.
Swear a tear does flow, your pen plunder.
Can't endear to Shakespeare, you're asunder.
You're effort's done, you'll never recover, yeah.

Getting your book represented by a big publisher requires finding an agent to pick you up first. It's not an easy task and it's tempting to kowtow to whatever the agent says when you get that close to landing a publishing deal. This author thinks very highly of her manuscript—and herself—and isn't going to be swayed by anyone!

TO THE TUNE OF

MATERIAL GIRL
MADONNA

Agents kiss me, agents hug me,
I think they're okay.
If they won't give me proper credit
I'll just walk away.

They can beg and they can plead
But they can't have the rights, no rights!
'Cause the book has such panache
The praise is mine, outright.

'Cause I have written a unique sequel
And I am a superior girl.

A self-published author isn't usually brimming with self-confidence. Nope. They're hoping and praying someone will buy their book and like it. Sing on…

TO THE TUNE OF

MANEATER
HALL & OATES

I only have time at night
To sit at my desk and type.
This manuscript's new,
It's like nothing I've read before.
Thinking, debating
Ooh, might I be through
Maybe I should write some more.

Nobody is paying me.
And don't you think
Self-publishing's free.
It took me a while
To pay the fees
Even had to sell my car.
Money don't matter.
If you're in it for cash
You ain't gonna get too far.

(Oh-oh, here they come)
Will they buy
or pass it up?
(Oh-oh, here they come)
They're my new readers.

(Oh-oh, here they come)
Will they buy
or pass it up?
(Oh-oh, here they come)
They're my new readers.

I just got a great review.
I know just what to do.
Cuz with my well-laid plan
My book's now in your shopping cart.
My heart's going patter.
Ooh, the sale is near.
Buy it now, be still my heart.

(Oh-oh, here they come)…

When an author updates a book, it's sometimes because they realize the first edition wasn't well written so they want to redeem themselves with the second edition. Apparently this new edition needed very few updates to make it fabulous!

LIKE A VIRGIN
MADONNA

I made it new, the manuscript.
Somehow I made it new.
Didn't know how bad it was until version two.
It was neat and complete. I'd been glad.
It was rad and cool, now it makes me reel.
Yeah, now I do feel that I hadn't a clue.

A new version.
Not like the very first time.
A new version.
All I did was change a few lines.

Gonna give you all the real McCoy.
My fear is fading fast.
Been changing it all for you, 'cause One is in the past.
They're so fine, these new lines.
Made 'em strong, yeah, they're new not old.
Oh, I rolled it out.
Yeah, I rolled it out, now it's being sold.

It takes a lot of work to get a book ready to print.
When it's nearly done, it's often hard to stop making changes
and let it go. Reaching that press day goal is a milestone!

RASPBERRY BERET
PRINCE

Yeah
I've been working full time saving every dime
Just to pay the printer's fee.
I wrote it several times now it's definitely time
To lock it up and throw out the key.

Seems that I was busy writing something
close to nothing
But different than the page before.
That's when it hit me, ooh it hit me
It was ready for the bookstore, bookstore.

And now it's finally press day.
We'll print a thousand, fill the shelves and the floor.
Finally press day.
And since it's the norm, we'll overprint a lot more.
Finally press day
Now I love it for sure.

*(Overprinting refers to the extra books that
often come off the press as it's shutting down.)*

WE GO TOGETHER

In this game, I've merged a book title with a song title using one common word. Fill in the blank and, if you're feeling like a teacher's pet, list the book's author and song's performer for extra credit.

HINT: Books are bestsellers and shown in italics. Songs from '70s and '80s.
(See page 12 for instructions.)

1) *How to Win Friends and Influence*

_____are People

Book's author _____

Song performed by _____

1) Love Plus _____*Flew Over the Cuckoo's Nest*

Book's author _____

Song performed by _____

3) Back in _____*Beauty*

Book's author _____

Song performed by _____

4) *The Old Man and the* _____of Love

Book's author _____

Song performed by _____

5) *Chicken Soup for the* _____Man

Book's authors_____

Song performed by _____

6) Sweet Baby _____*Bond*

Book's author _____

Song performed by _____

A Little Bit More…

7) You Can Do _____*Treehouse*

Book's author _____

Song performed by _____

8) *The Hardy* _____Don't Cry

Book's author _____

Song performed by _____

9) One of These _____*of Rain and Stars*

Book's author _____

Song performed by _____

10) I Wanna Be _____*Dad, Poor Dad*

Book's author _____

Song performed by _____

11) Black _____*Crocker Cookbook*

  Book's author _____

  Song performed by _____

12) My Sweet _____*of the Rings*

  Book's author _____

  Song performed by _____

13) The Most Beautiful _____*with the Dragon Tattoo*

  Book's author _____

  Song performed by _____

14) *A Wrinkle in* _____Passages

  Book's author _____

  Song performed by _____

Answers on page 96.

THE LOGICAL SONG

Let's assume for a few minutes that each of these musical artists is an author. Now let's get into their heads and determine how they might fill in these blanks.

Hint: All answers are song titles.

1) The time Robert Plant prefers to write:

When he's _____ _____ _____.

2) When Ronnie Milsap expects the first copy of his book to arrive in the mail:

_____ _____ _____

3) Kenny Rogers says this about the agent who works hard for him:

"_____ _____ _____."

4) What Milli Vanilli says when only five people show up for their book signing:

"_____ ____ ____ _____ _____."

5) What a forgiving Howard Jones says when he finds an error in his book:

"_____ _____ _____ _____ _____."

6) What Irene Cara is seeking from her writing career: _____.

7) Why Kajagoogoo declined to do an author interview:

They're _____ _____.

8) The ideal audience for Kim Carnes' new children's book about the USA:

_____ _____ _____ _____.

9) Where LL Cool J says he's heading on the first leg of his book tour:

"_____ _____ _____ _____."

10) How Men at Work's agent answers the phone when he receives their call:

"_____ _____ _____ _____ _____?"

Answers on pages 96–97.

Eat It

*If rock/pop stars wrote cookbooks,
what would they be titled?*

REASONS TO COOK

EXAMPLES: Hungry: Winger | **Breakfast in Bed**: Brenda K. Starr

Now it's your turn!

SONG   ARTIST

_____   _____

_____   _____

_____   _____

_____   _____

_____   _____

_____   _____

_____   _____

INGREDIENTS

EXAMPLES: **Fat**: Weird Al Yankovic | **Nobody's Dairy**: Yaz

Now it's your turn!

SONG   ARTIST

_____   _____

_____   _____

_____   _____

_____   _____

_____   _____

RECIPES

EXAMPLES: **Cherry Pie**: Warrant | **Popcorn Love**: New Edition

Now it's your turn!

SONG   ARTIST

_____   _____

_____   _____

A Little Bit More…

_____

_____

_____

_____

COOKING

EXAMPLES: Hot Hot Hot!!!: The Cure | **Stir it Up**: Patti LaBelle

Now it's your turn!

SONG   ARTIST

_____

_____

_____

_____

_____

_____

_____

DRINKS

EXAMPLES: **Have a Drink on Me**: AC/DC | **Wet My Whistle**: Midnight Star

Now it's your turn!

SONG

ARTIST

_____   _____

_____   _____

_____   _____

_____   _____

_____   _____

LET'S GO OUT TO EAT

EXAMPLES: **The Sad Cafe**: Eagles | **Tom's Diner**: DNA & Suzanne Vega

Now it's your turn!

SONG

ARTIST

_____   _____

_____   _____

A Little Bit More…

_____ _____

_____ _____

_____ _____

SWEETS

EXAMPLES: Bitter Sweet: Billy Ocean | **Candy Girl**: New Edition

Now it's your turn!

SONG   ARTIST

_____ _____

_____ _____

_____ _____

_____ _____

_____ _____

_____ _____

_____ _____

_____ _____

_____ _____

Crossroads

2) Rush's favorite fictional Tom.

4) Bob Seger says to do this to the page.

5) Earth, Wind and Fire would probably write this type of novel.

6) What Billy Joel feels when his publisher is pushing him to write another bestseller.

7) The type of novel Michael Jackson would've likely written.

8) What Run DMC would say about negotiating a detailed publisher's contract: "It's _____."

9) AC/DC has decided the color of this part of their book cover would be black.

10) What Survivor says when they finally find the perfect agent for their next book, "The _____ is Over."

DOWN

1) What Men at Work declares when they find an error in their manuscript, "It's a _____!"

3) People keep saying Robert Palmer's new book is simply this.

11) Wall of Voodoo wants to be interviewed about their book on this type of Mexican media.

Answers on page 97.

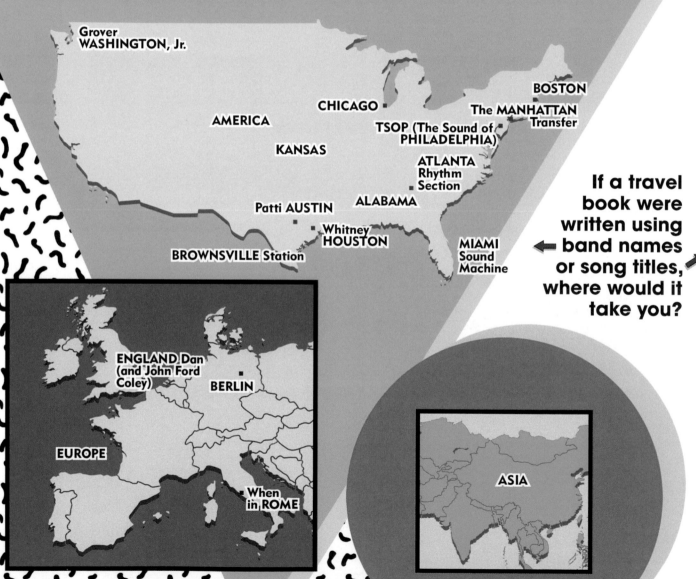

Somewhere OUT THERE

Grover WASHINGTON, Jr.

BOSTON

CHICAGO

The MANHATTAN Transfer

AMERICA

TSOP (The Sound of PHILADELPHIA)

KANSAS

ATLANTA Rhythm Section

Patti AUSTIN

ALABAMA

Whitney HOUSTON

MIAMI Sound Machine

BROWNSVILLE Station

If a travel book were written using ← band names or song titles, → where would it take you?

ENGLAND Dan (and John Ford Coley)

BERLIN

EUROPE

When in ROME

ASIA

SONGS THAT TAKE YOU THERE

WITHIN THE USA

Living in **America** (James Brown)

America (Neil Diamond)

For **America** (Jackson Browne)

New York Minute (Don Henley)

Englishman In **New York** (Sting)

No Sleep Till **Brooklyn** (Beastie Boys)

Angel of **Harlem** (U2)

Harlem Shuffle (Rolling Stones)

Woodstock (Crosby Stills and Nash)

Weekend in **New England** (Barry Manilow)

Philadelphia Freedom (Elton John)

Detroit Rock City (Kiss)

Key Largo (Bertie Higgins)

Kokomo (The Beach Boys)

The Devil Went Down to **Georgia** (Charlie Daniels Band)

Midnight Train to **Georgia** (Gladys Night and the Pips)

Sweet Home **Alabama** (Lynyrd Skynyrd)

City of **New Orleans** (Arlo Guthrie)

China Grove (Doobie Brothers)

La Grange (ZZ Top)

Tulsa Time (Eric Clapton)

Private **Idaho** (B-52's)

California Dreamin' (The Beach Boys)

California Girls (David Lee Roth)

Hotel **California** (Eagles)

Straight Outta **Compton** (N.W.A.)

L.A. Woman (Doors)

I Love **LA** (Randy Newman)

To Live and Die in **LA** (Wang Chung)

Walking In **L.A.** (Missing Persons)

Sausalito Summernight (Diesel)

Ventura Highway (America)

OUTSIDE THE USA

One Night in **Bangkok** (Murray Head)

Caribbean Queen (Billy Ocean)

China Girl (David Bowie)

China (Red Rockers)

Constantinople (Al Stewart)

Big In **Japan** (Alphaville)

Kashmir (Led Zeppelin)

Katmandu (Bob Seger)

London Calling (Clash)

London's Burning (Clash)

Werewolves of **London** (Warren Zevon)

Panama (Van Halen)

Rio (Duran Duran)

Woman from **Tokyo** (Deep Purple)

Waterloo (ABBA)

BILLY JOEL MAY BE THE ULTIMATE TOUR GUIDE, TAKING YOU TO: Allentown, Miami 2017 (Seen the Lights Go Out on **Broadway**), **New York** State of Mind, **Leningrad**, Good Night **Saigon**, **Vienna**, and **Zanzibar**.

Sign YOUR NAME

The band originally called The Sparrows

changed their name to Steppenwolf

after Herman Hesse's 1927 novel

at the suggestion of their producer.

MARKETING AND DISTRIBUTION

THE KEYS TO GET PEOPLE TO
NOTICE AND BUY
A BOOK

Publishing a book is a process with many moving parts—
some rewarding, some not-so-much.
This author is experiencing both.

TO THE TUNE OF

SWEET DREAMS (ARE MADE OF THIS)
EURYTHMICS

Sweet dreams are made of this.
Who am I to disagree?
I scribble the word and pay many fees.
Everybody's looking for something.
Distribution is the bane of me.
Everybody's looking for something.
Some of them want to use you.
Some of them return your books to you.
Some of them get some news for you.
Some of them buy one or two.

If nobody knows about your book, nobody buys it. Period. All (okay, most) authors dream of getting great publicity and fantastic reviews.

TO THE TUNE OF

I WANT A NEW DRUG
HUEY LEWIS & THE NEWS

I want a new plug, a book pitch that will stick.
One that won't make me seem subpar
or sound like a schtick.
I want a new plug, an idea that will spread.
One that will help me pay my bills
and keep my family fed.

One that will make me famous
And get me on the news.
One that helps me get five-star
Amazon reviews,
Amazon reviews.
Amazon reviews, yeah yeah.

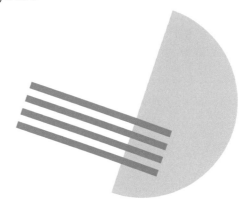

Ahh, the famed New York Times Bestseller List.
It's notoriously difficult to reach, yet worth striving for.

TO THE TUNE OF

PYT, MICHAEL JACKSON

I want to be there (N.Y.T.)
(Bestseller list).
Don't really care where (1-2-3)
(Bestseller list).
Review my book with flare.

Having an active online presence is a key way for authors
to reach their readers. Even after the book is out,
there's still more writing to do!

TO THE TUNE OF

HARD DAY'S NIGHT, BEATLES

It's been a hard day's night, and I've been working on my blog.
It's been a hard day's night, and my brain is in a fog.
Now Twitter, Facebook, too; I still have more things to do.
I think I'll be up all night.

(Yeah, this one's from the '60s, but it's timeless.)

Sign YOUR NAME

Actually, the name of the supergroup Bad English
isn't referring to grammar at all, but to the way
John Waite was playing pool one evening.
In the game of pool, "English" refers to hitting
the ball in a way that gives it sidespin.
Apparently he had a knack for that—
at least that night.

Selling foreign rights is how publishers license their books to be published in other countries. The London Book Fair is one of the biggest in the world and a good place for getting this process started. Here's a new twist on a well-known tune.

TO THE TUNE OF

SUMMER NIGHTS
OLIVIA NEWTON-JOHN
AND JOHN TRAVOLTA

London Book Fair,
had me a blast
You know it happened way too fast
Met a rep crazy for me
Rows of books far as I can see
All my fears are drifting away
'cause I sold foreign rights

Well-a, well-a, well-a, uh!
Tell me more, tell me more
Did you head to the bar?
Tell me more, tell me more
Can you buy a new car?

There are at least two large publishing-related competitions called the Benjamin Franklin Awards. This song was written specifically for the one put on by IBPA, the Independent Book Publishers Association. They host an annual ceremony celebrating outstanding books created by independent publishers nationwide.

TO THE TUNE OF

BENNIE AND THE JETS
ELTON JOHN

Authors, gather 'round together
So many nights of judging.
Did you remember to enter?
A feather in your cap tonight
So stick around.
You're gonna cheer each category
When it comes around.

Oh, gold and silver, have you seen them yet?
Oooh, but they're so decked out, B-B-B-Bennies are the best.
Oh and we'll cheer 'cause they're wonderful.
Oh Bennies are really keen.
They're going to introduce the winners soon.
You know I'm feeling the adrenaline.
Oh ohh, B-B-B-Bennies are the best.

WE GO TOGETHER
(CHILDREN'S BOOK EDITION)

In this game, I've merged a book title with a song title using one common word. Fill in the blank and, if you're feeling like a teacher's pet, list the book's author and song's performer for extra credit.

HINT: Books are bestsellers and shown in italics. Songs from the '70s and '80s.
(See page 12 for instructions.)

1) *The Littlest* _____ of Harlem

   Book's author _____

   Song performed by _____

2) *Hop on* _____ Goes the World

   Book's author _____

   Song performed by _____

3) *The Little Engine That* _____I Have This Dance

   Book's author _____

   Song performed by _____

4) *When We Were Very* _____Turks

   Book's author _____

   Song performed by _____

5) Our _____*at Pooh Corner*

   Book's author _____

   Song performed by _____

6) *Love You* _____Your Girl

   Book's author _____

   Song performed by _____

A Little Bit More…

7) *Chicka Chicka Boom* _____Boom

Book's authors_____

Song performed by _____

8) *Tales of a Fourth Grade* _____Compares 2 U

Book's author _____

Song performed by _____

9) Little by _____*House on the Prairie*

Book's author _____

Song performed by _____

10) Be Good _____*Tremain*

Book's author _____

Song performed by _____

11) *That Was Then, This Is*

_____That We Found Love

Book's author _____

Song performed by _____

12) *Stuart* _____Jeannie

Book's author _____

Song performed by _____

13) *The Call of the* _____Thing

Book's author _____

Song performed by _____

14) *Tuck* _____Love

Book's author _____

Song performed by _____

Answers on page 97.

THE LOGICAL SONG

Let's assume for a few minutes that each of these musical artists is an author. Now let's get into their heads and determine how they might fill in these blanks.

Hint: All answers are song titles.

1) What Michael Jackson does with the advertising poster when his book signing is finished: He takes it _____ _____ _____.

2) Nene decorates for her launch party with _____ _____ _____.

3) To get to his book signings, Ozzy Osbourne takes the _____ _____.

4) What The Clash is thinking when debating whether to go to the Frankfurt Book Fair: _____ ____ _____ ____ _____ ____ _____?

5) When asked how they feel about their bestselling author status, Loverboy responded with: "We're _____ _____ _____

_____ _____!"

6) How REO Speedwagon deals with the editing process:

They _____ _____ _____ _____.

7) The type of novel Earth, Wind and Fire would write: _____.

8) What Stephen Bishop says when he thinks he found the right agent:

"_____ _____ _____ _____."

9) What Madonna says to her father when he says he's not so sure about her becoming a full-time writer: "_____ _____ _____."

10) When asked if they enjoy being published authors, Poison answered, "We're having _____ _____ _____ _____ _____.

Answers on page 97.

WHAT DO YOU
Do For Money
HONEY?

If rock/pop stars wrote career books, what would they write about?

ON THE JOB

EXAMPLES: **9 To 5**: Dolly Parton | **Work It**: Teena Marie

Now it's your turn!

SONG   ARTIST

_____   _____

_____   _____

_____   _____

_____   _____

_____   _____

_____   _____

SPECIFIC JOB TITLES

EXAMPLES: Cab Driver: Daryl Hall | **Dream Police:** Cheap Trick

Now it's your turn!

SONG   ARTIST

_____   _____

_____   _____

_____   _____

_____   _____

_____   _____

_____   _____

_____   _____

_____   _____

_____   _____

_____   _____

A Little Bit More…

_____ _____

_____ _____

_____ _____

_____ _____

_____ _____

_____ _____

_____ _____

_____ _____

POLITICAL AND MILITARY CAREERS

EXAMPLES: Buffalo Soldier: Bob Marley & The Wailers | **Toy Soldiers**: Martika

Now it's your turn!

SONG   ARTIST

_____ _____

_____ _____

_____ _____

_____ _____

Crossroads

ACROSS

4) When George Michael couldn't meet his writing deadline,
   he said he was just Praying For _____.

6) Fans of Terence Trent D'Arby's latest book always say,
   "Sign Your _____" at his book signings.

7) When Billy Ocean was asked if his wife reads sci-fi, he said,
   "No, she's a _____ Lady."

8) When members of Golden Earring read a book they didn't realize
   they'd read before, they feel like they're in the Twilight _____.

9) The Escape Club's favorite pastime is reading about the _____, Wild West.

10) The Starland Vocal Band says reading at 2:30 pm is a real "_____ Delight."

DOWN

1) Stevie Ray Vaughan says his book is his _____ and Joy.

2) Cyndi Lauper had a Change of _____ and decided
   not to release her next book this year.

3) While in school, Eddie Van Halen's English teacher always said,
   "_____ What Ya Started!"

5) DJ Jazzy Jeff & The Fresh Prince like to read
   at the beach in the _____.

Answers on page 97.

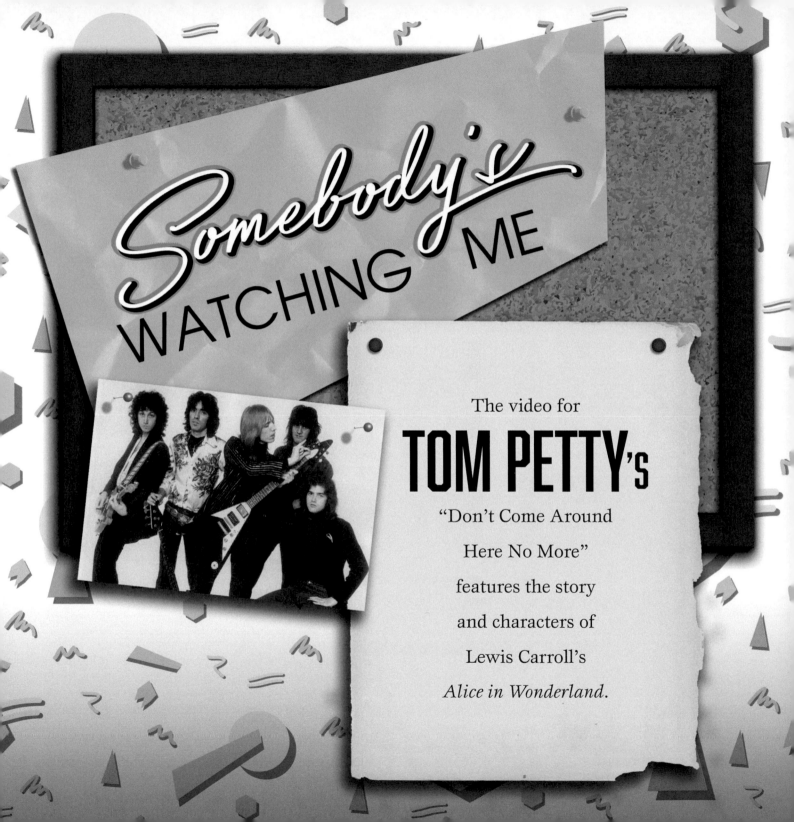

Somebody's WATCHING ME

The video for

TOM PETTY's

"Don't Come Around
Here No More"
features the story
and characters of
Lewis Carroll's
Alice in Wonderland.

In the video for "Head Over Heels" by

TEARS FOR FEARS,

Roland Orzabal is hanging out in the library,

trying to win over an unamused librarian.

Books abound! You'll have to watch it

to find out if he gets the girl.

CHANNEL

VOLUME

POWER

HEADPHONES

THIS ONE'S FOR THE
Children

SONG TITLES THAT WOULD MAKE GOOD CHILDREN'S BOOKS

ABC by The Jackson 5

That's What Friends are For by Dionne & Friends

I Wanna Be a Cowboy by Boys Don't Cry

Playing With the Boys by Kenny Loggins

Little Jackie Wants to Be a Star by Lisa Lisa & Cult Jam

Little Dreamer by Van Halen

Dance Little Sister by Terence Trent D'Arby

Another One Rides the Bus by Weird Al Yankovic

Don't Talk to Strangers by Rick Springfield

Sweet Child o' Mine by Guns N' Roses

Hide and Seek by Howard Jones

WHAT YOU
Don't Know
*Better known
as the answer key.*

WE GO TOGETHER, PG 12

1) Beauty / Gabrielle-Suzanne Barbot de Villeneuve / The Tubes . . . .

2) Small / James Herriot / John Mellencamp

3) Jungle / Rudyard Kipling / Guns N' Roses

4) Rich / Napoleon Hill / Hall and Oates

5) Flowers / V. C. Andrews / Neil Diamond (and Barbara Streisand)

6) Down / Richard Adams / Men at Work

7) Gone / Margaret Mitchell / Eagles

8) Games / Suzanne Collins / The Alan Parsons Project

9) Stars / John Green / Stars On 45

10) Train / Paula Hawkins / Clash

11) Animal / George Orwell / James Ingram

12) Pride / Jane Austen / Darryl Hall

13) Secret / Rhonda Byrne / Night Ranger

14) Life / Yann Martel / Debby Boone

THE LOGICAL SONG, PG 16

1) Sweet Dreams (Are Made Of This)

2) I Just Wanna Stop

3) So Far So Good

4) Don't You Forget About Me

5) Drive

6) No Reply At All

7) I Just Called to Say I Love You

8) Don't Let it End

9) Should've Known Better

10) Ain't Too Proud to Beg

CROSSROADS, PG 24

ACROSS

1) Carry

2) Rain

4) Once

95

CROSSROADS, PG 24
(CONTINUED)
6) Tight
9) Centipede
10) Jet
11) Psalms

DOWN
1) Claire
3) Forever
5) Nightshift
8) New
9) Cherish

THE LOGICAL SONG, PG 34
1) Hold Me Now
2) (Just Like) Starting Over
3) You Can't Change That
4) Cover Girl
5) Another One Bites the Dust
6) Here I Go Again
7) On The Road Again
8) Cool Change
9) Release Me
10) Take Me Home Tonight

CROSSROADS, PG 40
ACROSS
1) Sorry
2) Hello
4) Page
5) Science
8) Michael
9) ending
10) Someday
12) Jane

DOWN
1) Superwoman
3) Overjoyed
6) Coffee
7) Superman
11) Alphabet

WE GO TOGETHER, PG 56
1) People / Dale Carnegie / Depeche Mode
2) One / Ken Kesey / Haircut One Hundred
3) Black / Anna Sewell / AC/DC
4) Sea / Ernest Hemingway / Honeydrippers (or Del Shannon)
5) Soul / Jack Canfield and Mark Victor Hansen / Blues Brothers
6) James / Ian Fleming / James Taylor
7) Magic / Mary Pope Osborne / America
8) Boys / (pseudonym) Franklin W. Dixon / The Cure
9) Nights / Maeve Binchy / Eagles
10) Rich / Robert Kiyosaki (and Sharon Lechter) / Calloway
11) Betty / staff at General Mills / Ram Jam
12) Lord / J. R. R. Tolkien / George Harrison
13) Girl / Stieg Larsson / Charlie Rich
14) Time / Madeleine L'Engle / Al Stewart

THE LOGICAL SONG, PG 60
1) In the Mood
2) Any Day Now
3) She Believes in Me
4) Blame it on the Rain
5) No One is to Blame

6) Fame

7) Too Shy

8) The Kids in America

9) Going Back to Cali

10) Who Can it Be Now?

CROSSROADS, PG 68

ACROSS

2) Sawyer

4) Turn

5) Fantasy

6) Pressure

7) Thriller

8) Tricky

9) Back

10) Search

DOWN

1) Mistake

3) Irresistible

11) Radio

WE GO TOGETHER, PG 80

1) Angel / Charles Tazewell / U2

2) Pop / Dr. Seuss / Men Without Hats

3) Could / Watty Piper / Anne Murray

4) Young / A.A. Milne / Rod Stewart

5) House / A.A. Milne / Madness

6) Forever / Robert Munsch / Paula Abdul

7) Boom / Bill Martin Jr. and John Archambault / Paul Lekakis

8) Nothing / Judy Blume / Sinead O'Connor

9) Little / Laura Ingalls Wilder / Robert Plant

10) Johnny / Esther Forbes / Men at Work

11) Now / S.E. Hinton / Heavy D & The Boyz

12) Little / E.B. White / Elton John

13) Wild / Jack London / Tone Loc

14) Everlasting / Natalie Babbitt / Howard Jones

THE LOGICAL SONG, PG 84

1) Off The Wall

2) 99 Red Balloons (or 99 Luftballoons)

3) Crazy Train

4) Should I Stay or Should I Go

5) Nothin' but a Good Time

6) Roll With the Changes

7) Fantasy

8) It Might Be You

9) Papa Don't Preach

10) Lovin' Every Minute of It

CROSSROADS, PG 90

ACROSS

4) Time

6) Name

7) Mystery

8) Zone

9) Wild

10) Afternoon

DOWN

1) Pride

2) Heart

3) Finish

4) Summertime

EVERYBODY'S GOT TO LEARN

*Did you notice that most of the major headings
(and a few other fun instances) throughout this book
are also song titles? Just in case you don't recall the artist
who made each famous, here's a list to settle your mind.*

iii) Where Do We Go From Here,
Stacy Lattisaw & Johnny Gill

v) We're in This Love Together,
Al Jarreau

vi) Ready or Not, Bananarama

Let's Go, The Cars or Wang Chung

Come On, Let's Go, Los Lobos

Nothing's Going to Stop Us Now,
Starship

1) Does Your Mother Know, ABBA

6) Word Up, Cameo (also on page 44)

12) We Go Together, Olivia Newton-John
and John Travolta (also on pages
56, 80)

16) The Logical Song, Supertramp
(also on pages 34, 60, 84)

18) Dr. Feelgood, Motley Crue

24) Crossroads, Tracy Chapman
(also on pages 40, 68, 90)

26) Sign Your Name,
Terence Trent D'Arby
(also on pages 31, 49, 72, 77)

36) What a Wonderful World,
Louis Armstrong

EXTRA: At the bottom of the game pages when it continues to another page: A Little Bit More, Dr. Hook (also by Melba Moore & Freddie Jackson)

DID YOU NOTICE? This book contains three songs with new lyrics that were originally released before or after the 1970–1989 timeframe. Can you name them?

A LITTLE BIT MORE

Bibliographical resources

AZLyrics.com

bookriot.com/2016/07/26/29-popular-songs-reference-classic-books

discjockey.org/top-100-songs-of-the-1970s

en.wikipedia.org/wiki/List_of_band_name_etymologies

en.wikipedia.org/wiki/List_of_best-selling_books

en.wikipedia.org/wiki/List_of_songs_that_retell_a_work_of_literature

FlashbackRadio.com

Genius.com

MetroLyrics.com

PublishersWeekly.com

puzzlemaker.discoveryeducation.com

RhymeZone.com

shortlist.com/entertainment/music/25-songs-that-reference-books/78348

Songfacts.com

VIDEO KILLED THE RADIO STAR

*Links to the videos featured in the
"Somebody's Watching Me" sidebars.*

Toto, Africa: www.youtube.com/watch?v=FTQbiNvZqaY

A-Ha, Take On Me: https://youtu.be/djV11Xbc914

Tom Petty, Don't Come Around Here No More, www.youtube.com/watch?v=h0JvF9vpqx8

Tears for Fears, Head Over Heels, www.youtube.com/watch?v=CsHiG-43Fzg

YOU GOTTA FIGHT FOR YOUR RIGHT

Art and photo credits and copyrights

Thank You
FOR BEING A FRIEND

Thanks to my **Somebody to Love**, Tom, for loving me despite my crazy obsessions, singing around the house though I'm no pro, and dealing with me coming up with lyrics no matter where or when. I love you so! To Brett for putting up with Mom listening to "old" music at home and in the car and blurting out lyrics mid-conversation because they happen to fit right in. You may not think I'm cool now, but one day you'll realize that I am. (A mom can dream, right?) To Hope for joining in the musical fun and games and starting to follow in my footsteps. (Sorry/not sorry to her future husband!)

Erin Stark & Monica Thomas, you're two of my best friends and my cohorts at TLC. You've joined in my crazy lyrics quizzes and rewrites for years, yet still love me and we continue to work together. Your support is priceless. I don't have words for how wonderful this ride together has been so far!

To IBPA and specifically Angela Bole for indulging in my crazy lyrics and helping me share these songs with other book lovers. I love that you love these as much as I do! To Bob Baker for upgrading several of my songs. Thanks for supporting my creative habit and sharing your musical talent along this silly journey. Joe Bissen, thanks for trading music puns, your editorial support, and for being a totally-cool uncle with great taste in music.

Misti Moyer, thank you for your generous, thorough editing prowess. Lisa Pelto, your publishing expertise, sense of humor, and giving spirit have kept me relatively sane throughout! You are both valued friends!

Mom and Dad, thank you for instilling in me a love for books, as well as encouraging my design career. Daddy, I love that you were always playing music and knew the name of every singer. Now I do the same with your grandkids.

Jesus, You are the author of all and my everything. My life came into focus when you became my focus. You've led my career and created me to create. Most of all, You've given me the promise of a perfect, eternal life with You, the ultimate Creator. Thank you would never be enough. I can't wait to hug You in person.

My love to you all!

Jam

Something
ABOUT YOU

Tamara (call her Tami or Tam) Dever grew up on books, music, and art. She began reading at a very early age and read every horse book available from the library or the Arrow Book Club. Her dad had her convinced that country was the only type of real music until she discovered pop in sixth grade. In fact, while in junior high, her first concert was to see Johnny Cash with her family. She still loves the nostalgia classic country brings, but prefers '70s and '80s rock and pop these days.

Tami is the founder and creative director of TLC Book Design, a leading, boutique book creation firm for publishers of all sizes. She's somewhat addicted to playing lyrics trivia games with her coworkers (or anyone who will join the fun) and has an epic '80s costume birthday party each year. Concerts are her favorite thing to do on a date night and she's seen Billy Joel eleven times, including at Lambeau Field—a thrill for a die-hard Packer fan! Other favorites include Queen, Journey, Styx, Chicago, and Toto. She'll insert a fitting lyric into any conversation and can rewrite a song with lyrics that'll make you laugh (or roll your eyes) in minutes. (You read the book, right? Tell me they didn't roll at least once.)

Tamara lives in Austin, Texas with her husband, two kids, two dogs, and a boatload of books, cassettes, albums, and CDs.

DON'T DREAM IT'S OVER

No, really,

THE PARTY'S OVER

Seriously,

THAT'S ALL

I mean it,

ENOUGH IS ENOUGH

That's it. There are

NO MORE WORDS

*(What? Too much? **Overkill**?)*